Best Homemade Mac and Cheese Recipes

Comfort Foods - Macaroni and Cheese

Diana Loera

Copyright 2015 All rights reserved
Without limiting the rights under the copyright reserved above, no part of this book may be reproduced, stored in or introduced into a retrieval system, or transmitted, in any form, or by any means (electronic, mechanical, photocopying, recording, or otherwise) without the prior written permission of Diana Loera and Loera Publishing LLC.

Book piracy and any other forms of unauthorized distribution or use without written permission by Diana Loera/Loera Publishing LLC will be prosecuted to the fullest extent of the law.

Table of Contents

Other Books by Diana Loera 4
Introduction 5
Chipotle Mac and Cheese 6
Bacon-Pear Macaroni and Cheese 7
Slow-Cooker Mac & Cheese 10
Broccoli Macaroni and Cheese 12
Chicken, Tomato and Spinach Mac and Cheese 14
Cheeseburger Mac and Cheese 15
Tex-Mex Mac and Cheese 16
Army and Lou's Macaroni and Cheese 17
Butternut Squash Mac and Cheese 18
Mexican Mac and Cheese 20
Greek Style Mac and Cheese 21
Pesto Shrimp Mac & Cheese 22
Chicken-Broccoli Mac and Cheese 24
Pumpkin Mac and Cheese 25
Lobster Macaroni and Cheese 26

Other Books by Diana Loera

12 Extra Special Summer Dessert Fondue Recipes   http://tinyurl.com/q7gpgw8

14 Extra Special Winter Holidays Fondue Recipes   http://tinyurl.com/lkebggx

Awesome Thanksgiving Leftovers Revive Guide   http://tinyurl.com/prxjayg

Best 100 Calorie or Less Dessert Recipes http://tinyurl.com/pn5b46c

Best Bacon Infused Dessert Recipes: 20 Mouthwatering Delicious Desserts Infused with Bacon http://tinyurl.com/owxo3pl

Best Copycat Recipes on the Planet http://tinyurl.com/pcuj24q

Coca Cola Ham, Coca Cola Cake and Other Coca Cola Recipes http://tinyurl.com/pp2wvhz

Party Time Chicken Wing Recipes   http://tinyurl.com/ohsc9x8

Summertime Sangria   http://tinyurl.com/oxnlnhm

Please visit www.LoeraPublishingLLC.com to see our complete selection of books. Topics include cooking, travel, recipes, how to, non- fiction and more.

Introduction

Macaroni and cheese brings back favorite childhood memories and in my case, memories of when my daughter was quite young as she loved macaroni and cheese.

A few years ago while dining at a restaurant in Boston, I had a side dish of lobster macaroni and cheese. That was when the light bulb went off in my head that there were probably a lot of great recipes using macaroni and cheese.

Macaroni and cheese is typically thought of as a comfort food and also a budget friendly food.

But what if we took mac and cheese a step further and jazzed it up a bit? We can have a side dish or main dish that is suitable for family night or entertaining.

In this book you'll find an array of, in my opinion, the best homemade mac and cheese variations. From mac and cheese to pumpkin mac and cheese to lobster mac and cheese, there are recipes sure to please.

All of my recipe books are an oversized 8 ½ x 11 in size. I hate squinting at tiny print and trying to use a tiny recipe book while cooking and don't feel you should have to do so either.

I have included some color photos but every color photo that I add drives up the book cost so I try to be very selective – thank you for understanding.

Thank you for taking the time to read through my recipes. I hope you find a favorite or two in this book.

Sincerely,

Diana

Chipotle Mac and Cheese

Prep 25 mins
Bake 30 mins
Stand 10 mins

Ingredients:

12 ounces dried medium shell pasta
2 tablespoons butter
2 tablespoons all-purpose flour
1 12 - ounce can evaporated milk
1 cup milk
1 1/2 cups shredded Monterey Jack cheese (6 ounces)
1 1/2 cups shredded sharp cheddar cheese (6 ounces)
1 tablespoon chopped canned chipotle pepper in adobo sauce
1/4 teaspoon salt
1 pound bulk pork sausage or uncooked chorizo sausage, cooked and drained, or 2 cups diced cooked ham

Directions:

1. Preheat oven to 350 degrees F. Lightly grease a 2- to 2 1/2-quart casserole; set aside. Cook pasta according to package directions; drain. Return to pan.

2. Meanwhile, in a medium saucepan melt butter over medium heat. Stir in flour; cook and stir for 1 minute. Gradually stir in evaporated milk and milk. Cook and stir until slightly thickened and bubbly. Remove from heat. Stir in 1 cup of the Monterey Jack cheese, 1 cup of the cheddar cheese, the chipotle pepper, and salt. Stir cheese mixture into cooked pasta. Stir in cooked sausage.

3. Transfer mixture to the prepared casserole. Sprinkle with the remaining 1/2 cup Monterey Jack cheese and the remaining 1/2 cup cheddar cheese. Place casserole on a baking sheet. Bake, covered, about 30 minutes or until bubbly. Let stand for 10 minutes before serving.

Bacon-Pear Macaroni and Cheese

Prep 40 mins
Bake 30 mins
Stand 10 mins

Ingredients:

8 ounces dried elbow macaroni (2 cups) or other short tubular pasta (2 1/3 cups)
6 slices bacon
1/2 cup chopped onion (1 medium)
2 cloves garlic, minced
2 tablespoons all-purpose flour
1 teaspoon dry mustard
1/2 teaspoon freshly ground black pepper
2 1/2 cups whole milk
6 ounces smoked Gouda cheese, rind removed and shredded
1 8 - ounce package cream cheese, cubed and softened
2 tablespoons snipped fresh oregano or 1 teaspoon dried oregano, crushed
2 tablespoons butter or margarine
2 tablespoons packed brown sugar
2 red and/or green pears, thinly sliced
2 tablespoons finely shredded Parmesan cheese

Directions:

1. Cook pasta according to package directions; drain. Return pasta to hot pan; cover to keep warm. Set aside.

2. Meanwhile, in a large skillet, cook bacon over medium heat until crisp, turning once. Drain bacon on paper towels, reserving 3 tablespoons bacon drippings in skillet. Crumble and set aside. Reserve 3 tablespoons bacon drippings in skillet.

3. Cook onion and garlic in bacon drippings over medium heat for 30 seconds. Stir in flour, dry mustard and pepper. Add milk all at once. Cook and stir until thickened and bubbly; reduce heat. Add smoked Gouda cheese and cream cheese; cook and stir until almost melted.

4. Pour cheese sauce over the cooked pasta. Stir in oregano and all but 2 tablespoons of the crumbled bacon. Transfer mixture to an ungreased to 2-quart rectangular baking dish; cover with foil. Bake in a 350 degrees oven for 25 minutes.

5. Meanwhile, melt butter in a clean, large skillet. Stir in brown sugar; add pear slices. Cook, turning occasionally, until pears are tender, about 6 to 8 minutes. Remove from heat. Remove foil from the baking dish. Stir about half of the cooked, sliced pears into the macaroni and cheese. Spoon the remaining pear slices atop macaroni and cheese; sprinkle with Parmesan and reserved crumbled bacon. Return to oven and bake 5 minutes or until Parmesan has softened. Let stand 10 minutes before serving.

Bacon-Pear Macaroni and Cheese

Slow-Cooker Mac & Cheese

Prep 15 mins
Cook 2 mins
Slow Cook 3 hrs on HIGH
Slow Cook 4 hrs on LOW

Ingredients:

10 ounce (2 1/4 cups) dry elbow macaroni
1 cup shredded cheddar cheese
1 cup shredded Gruyere cheese
8 ounces American cheese, thinly sliced and roughly chopped
1 1/2 cups milk
1 12 - ounce can evaporated milk
1 1/2 teaspoons Worcestershire sauce
3/4 teaspoon dry mustard
1/4 teaspoon salt
1/4 teaspoon black pepper
1 tablespoon unsalted butter
1/2 cup panko bread crumbs

Directions:

1. Coat inside of slow-cooker bowl with nonstick cooking spray.

2. Combine macaroni, cheddar, Gruyere and American cheeses,
milk and evaporated milk in slow-cooker bowl; stir well and cover; cook on HIGH for 3 hours or LOW for 4 hours.

3. When there is 30 minutes cook time remaining, stir in Worcestershire, mustard, salt and pepper.

4. Melt butter in a small nonstick skillet over medium-high heat. Stir in panko and cook, stirring often, for 2 minutes or until toasted and golden. Sprinkle over Mac & Cheese and serve immediately.

Slow-Cooker Mac & Cheese

Broccoli Macaroni and Cheese

Yield: 9 cups
Hands on 30 mins
Total Time 55 mins

Ingredients:

7 ounces Swiss cheese, shredded (1 3/4 cup)
7 ounces mild cheddar cheese, shredded (1 3/4 cup)
2 1/2 cups dried elbow macaroni
3 cups bite-size broccoli florets
2/3 cup chopped onion
2 tablespoons butter
2 tablespoons all-purpose flour
1/4 teaspoon ground black pepper
3 cups milk
2 tablespoons butter, melted
1/3 cup fine dry bread crumbs
1/4 cup grated Parmesan cheese

Directions:

1. Let both cheese stand at room temperature for 30 minutes.

2. Cook macaroni in a large pot according to package directions until tender, but still firm, adding broccoli during the last 5 minutes of cooking. Drain well and return to pot; set aside.

3. Meanwhile, in a medium saucepan, cook the onion in the 3 tablespoons butter until tender but not brown. Stir in the flour and the pepper. Add the milk all at once. Cook and stir until the mixture is slightly thickened and bubbly. Remove from heat. Gradually add both cheeses, stirring until melted (the mixture will appear slightly curdled). Pour over the macaroni and broccoli and stir gently to combine. Transfer mixture to a 2 1/2- to 3-quart baking dish.

4. In a small bowl combine melted butter, bread crumbs, and Parmesan cheese. Toss to coat. Sprinkle over the macaroni mixture.

5. Bake in a 350 degrees F oven about 20 minutes or until heated through. Let stand for 5 minutes before serving.

Broccoli Macaroni and Cheese

Chicken, Tomato and Spinach Mac and Cheese

Makes: 8 servings
Yield: 10 cups
Start to Finish 45 mins

Ingredients:

2 cups dry elbow macaroni (8 ounces)
1 purchased roasted chicken
1 tablespoon butter
2/3 cup panko bread crumbs
2 1/2 cups half-and-half, light cream or whipping cream
6 ounces sharp cheddar cheese, shredded (1 1/2 cups)
4 ounces American cheese slices, torn
4 ounces fontina or Havarti cheese, shredded (1 cup)
1/8 teaspoon ground black pepper
2 medium tomatoes, seeded and chopped
2 cups coarsely chopped fresh spinach
1 tablespoon snipped fresh oregano

Directions:

1. In a 4- to 6-quart Dutch oven, cook macaroni according to package directions. Drain and set aside.

2. Meanwhile, remove the meat from the chicken; discard skin and bones. Coarsely shred the chicken; set aside.

3. For the topping: In a medium skillet melt butter over medium heat. Add panko. Cook and stir until panko is lightly toasted. Remove from the heat and set aside.

4. Add half-and-half to the same Dutch oven used to cook the macaroni. Bring just to a simmer over medium heat. Reduce heat to medium-low. Gradually add cheddar, American and fontina cheeses, stirring constantly. Stir in black pepper. Continue to cook and stir until cheese is completely melted and smooth.

5. Add drained macaroni to the cheese sauce. Stir until well combined. Stir in chicken and tomatoes. Cook and stir for 1 to 2 minutes or until heated through. Remove from the heat. Stir in spinach and oregano. Serve immediately, topped with toasted panko mixture.

Cheeseburger Mac and Cheese

Prep 10 mins
Cook 10 mins
Bake 20 mins
Broil 2 mins

Ingredients:

1 box (1 pound) elbow macaroni or rotini
1 pound ground sirloin
1/2 teaspoon salt
1/4 teaspoon black pepper
1/4 cup ketchup
2 tablespoons yellow mustard
1 tablespoon unsalted butter
1 tablespoon all-purpose flour
1 can (12 ounces) evaporated milk
3 cups shredded cheddar cheese
2 medium-size tomatoes, cored and thinly sliced
2 tablespoons seasoned bread crumbs

Directions:

1. Heat oven to 350 degrees F. Coat a 2-quart oval baking dish with nonstick cooking spray.

2. Bring a large pot of lightly salted water to boiling. Add pasta and cook 10 minutes, according to package directions. Drain.

3. While pasta cooks, heat a large nonstick skillet over medium-high heat. Add sirloin, breaking apart with a wooden spoon. Cook 6 minutes, until no longer pink. Season with 1/4 teaspoon of the salt and the pepper. Remove from heat and stir in ketchup and mustard. Transfer to a bowl.

4. Return skillet to medium heat and add butter. Once melted, whisk in flour, then add milk in a thin stream. Bring to a simmer and cook 2 minutes. Remove from heat and whisk in remaining 1/4 teaspoon salt and 2 cups of the cheese. Stir in pasta. Pour into prepared dish. Top with meat mixture, remaining cheese, sliced tomatoes and bread crumbs. Spritz with nonstick cooking spray.

5. Bake at 350 degrees F for 20 minutes. Increase heat to broil and broil for 2 minutes.

Tex-Mex Mac and Cheese

Makes: 10 servings
Prep 20 mins
Slow Cook 5 hrs to 6 hrs (low)

Ingredients:

2 pounds lean ground beef
1 large onion, chopped
3 cups shredded Mexican-blend cheese (12 ounces)
1 16 - ounce jar salsa
1 15 - ounce jar cheese dip
1 4 - ounce can diced green chile peppers, undrained
1 2 1/4 - ounce can sliced, pitted ripe olives, drained
12 ounces dried elbow macaroni

Directions:

1. In a large skillet, cook ground beef and onion until meat is brown and onion is tender. Drain off fat. Transfer meat mixture to a 4 1/2- to 6-quart slow cooker. Add Mexican-blend cheese, salsa, cheese dip, undrained chile peppers, and olives; stir to combine.

2. Cover; cook on low-heat setting for 5 1/2 to 6 hours (do not use high-heat setting).

3. Cook macaroni according to package directions; drain. Stir macaroni into mixture in cooker.

Army and Lou's Macaroni and Cheese

I live close to Chicago and I'll say, forget all the crowing about chicken and waffles, Army and Lou's Soul Food Mac and Cheese will have your family and friends begging for seconds. From the Windy City to your table – here is their famous recipe. This much loved restaurant was open from the mid 1940's until 2011 and was a well- known Chicago icon.

Prep 25 mins
Bake 40 mins to 45 mins
Stand 10 mins

Ingredients:

16 ounces dried elbow macaroni (4 cups)
1 8 - ounce package shredded sharp cheddar cheese (2 cups)
1 8 - ounce package pasteurized prepared cheese product, cut up
1/4 cup butter, cut cup
3 eggs, lightly beaten
1 12 - ounce can evaporated milk
1 cup process cheese dip or 1 10.75-ounce can condensed cheddar cheese soup
1/4 teaspoon ground white pepper

Directions:

1. Cook macaroni according to package directions. Meanwhile, let the cheeses and butter stand at room temperature. Drain macaroni; transfer to a very large bowl. Add 1-1/2 cups of the shredded cheddar, the cheese product, and the butter to the hot pasta, stirring well. Set aside.

2. In a medium bowl, whisk together eggs, milk, cheese dip, and white pepper until combined. Stir egg mixture into macaroni mixture. Transfer mixture to a 13x9x2-inch baking dish (3-quart rectangular) spreading evenly.

3. Bake, covered, in a 325 degree F oven for 25 minutes. Uncover and stir well. Sprinkle with the remaining 1/2 cup shredded cheddar. Bake, uncovered, 15 to 20 minutes more or until cheese is melted and mixture is heated through (160 degrees F). Let stand 10 minutes before serving. Makes 8 to 10 servings.

Butternut Squash Mac and Cheese

My friend since 7th grade, Jeannette, loves squash so when she told me she had a recipe that married her favorite vegetable, squash, with mac and cheese, I was ready to do a taste test. This recipe while great for family night is also great for entertaining and for potlucks. Be sure to make copies of the recipe as people will ask you for it.

Prep 15 mins
Bake 14 mins to 15 mins
Cook 40 mins to 47 mins

Ingredients:

12 ounces dried rigatoni
1 1/2 pounds butternut squash, peeled, seeded and cut into chunks (3 1/2 cups)
2 3/4 cups milk
1/4 cup all-purpose flour
8 ounces smoked Gruyere cheese, shredded (2 cups)
8 slices bacon
2 small sweet onions, cut into chunks
3 ounces sourdough bread
2 tablespoons butter, melted
Fresh flat-leaf Italian parsley

Directions:

1. Preheat the oven to 425 degrees F. Lightly butter a 3-quart au gratin or baking dish; set aside. Cook pasta according to package directions. Drain; transfer to a large bowl.

2. Meanwhile, in a large saucepan combine the squash and 2 1/2 cups of the milk over medium-high heat. Bring to boiling; reduce heat to medium, and simmer until the squash is tender when pierced with a fork, 18 to 20 minutes. Stir together remaining 1/4 cup milk and flour; stir into squash mixture. Bring to boiling; cook until thickened, 2 to 3 minutes. Stir in 1 1/2 cups of the Gruyere until melted; keep warm.

3. Meanwhile, in a very large skillet cook bacon until crisp; drain on paper towels. Crumble; set aside. Pour off all but 2 tablespoons bacon drippings. Return skillet to the heat.

4. Add onions to skillet; cover and cook over low heat 10 minutes, stirring occasionally. Uncover and increase heat to high. Cook 4 to 6 minutes more, stirring, until onions are golden.

5. Add squash-cheese mixture, onions, and bacon to the bowl with the pasta. Toss well to combine, then transfer to prepared baking dish.

6. Place bread in a food processor and pulse with two or three on/off turns to form large coarse crumbs (you should have about 2 cups). Transfer to a small bowl; mix with melted butter. Sprinkle remaining Gruyere and the bread crumbs over pasta mixture. Oven bake until top is browned, about 14 to 15 minutes. Cool 5 minutes. Sprinkle with parsley. Makes 6 to 8 servings.

Mexican Mac and Cheese

Prep 20 mins
Bake 35 mins
Stand 10 mins

Ingredients:

12 ounces dried mostaccioli or rigatoni pasta (3 cups)
1 pound bulk pork sausage
1 cup chopped onion
1 16 - ounce jar green medium-hot salsa
2 8 - ounce package shredded Monterey Jack cheese (4 cups)
Tomato wedges, sliced jalapeno peppers, and chopped fresh cilantro
Salsa (optional)

Directions:

1. Preheat oven to 350 degrees F. Lightly grease 3-quart rectangular baking dish; set aside. Cook pasta according to package directions. Drain; set aside.

2. Meanwhile, in large skillet cook sausage and onion until meat is browned and onion is tender. Drain fat, return sausage and onion to skillet. Stir in green salsa.

3. In prepared baking dish layer half of the cooked pasta, half the sausage mixture, and half the cheese. Repeat layers. Bake, uncovered, for 35 minutes or until bubbly. Let stand 10 minutes. Top with tomato, jalapeno, and cilantro. If desired, serve with additional salsa. Makes 12 servings.

Greek Style Mac and Cheese

Prep 25 mins
Bake 25 mins to 30 mins
Stand 10 mins

Ingredients:

2 cups packaged dried elbow macaroni (8 ounces)
1/2 cup chopped onion (1 medium)
2 tablespoons butter or margarine
2 tablespoons all-purpose flour
1/8 teaspoon ground black pepper
2 1/2 cups milk
1 1/2 cups shredded cheddar cheese (6 ounces)
1 1/2 cups shredded American cheese (6 ounces)
1/2 cup pitted Kalamata olives, halved
2 tablespoons crumbled feta cheese
Snipped fresh oregano

Directions:

1. Cook macaroni according to package directions; drain. Set aside.

2. Meanwhile, preheat oven to 350 degrees F. For cheese sauce, in a medium saucepan cook onion in hot butter until tender. Stir in flour and pepper. Add milk all at once. Cook and stir over medium heat until slightly thickened and bubbly. Add cheeses, stirring until melted. Stir in cooked macaroni and olives. Transfer mixture to an ungreased 2-quart casserole.

3. Bake, uncovered, for 25 to 30 minutes or until bubbly. Top with feta cheese and oregano. Let stand for 10 minutes before serving.

Pesto Shrimp Mac & Cheese

Prep 20 mins
Bake 40 mins
Stand 10 mins

Ingredients:

1 pound fresh or frozen medium shrimp in shells
8 ounces dried elbow macaroni (2 cups)
2 eggs, lightly beaten
1/4 cup butter, melted
1 cup half-and-half
1 1/4 cups shredded fontina cheese (5 oz.)
1/2 cup grated Parmesan cheese
2 cloves garlic, minced
2 tablespoons pine nuts, toasted
1 1/2 cups lightly packed fresh basil leaves, chopped
Fresh basil leaves

Directions:

1. Thaw shrimp, if frozen. Preheat oven to 350 degrees F. Peel and devein shrimp, removing tails. Rinse shrimp; pat dry with paper towels. Chop shrimp and set aside.

2. Cook macaroni according to package directions. Drain and keep warm.

3. In large bowl stir together eggs, butter, half-and-half, 1 cup of the fontina cheese, 1/4 cup of the Parmesan cheese, garlic, pine nuts, chopped basil, and 1/4 teaspoon each salt and pepper. Stir in shrimp and macaroni. Transfer to buttered 2-quart casserole. Top with remaining cheeses.

4. Bake, uncovered, 40 to 45 minutes or until heated through and shrimp pieces are opaque. Let stand for 10 minutes before serving. Top with fresh basil leaves. Makes 6 servings.

Pesto Shrimp Mac & Cheese

Chicken-Broccoli Mac and Cheese

Makes: 4 servings
Start to Finish 21 mins

Ingredients:

8 ounces dried rigatoni
2 cups fresh broccoli florets
1 2 - 2 1/4 - pound whole roasted chicken
1 5.2 - ounce package semisoft cheese with garlic and fine herbs
3/4-1 cup milk
1/4 cup oil-packed dried tomatoes, drained and snipped
1/4 teaspoon freshly ground black pepper
Fresh Italian (flat-leaf) parsley, optional

Directions:

1. In large saucepan cook pasta according to package directions, adding broccoli florets during the last 3 minutes of cooking time. While pasta is cooking, remove meat from roasted chicken. Coarsely chop chicken. Drain pasta and broccoli; set aside.

2. In same saucepan combine cheese, the 3/4 cup milk, tomatoes, and 1/4 teaspoon freshly ground black pepper. Cook and stir until cheese is melted. Add pasta mixture and chicken. Heat through. If necessary, thin with additional milk. Sprinkle fresh parsley. Makes 4 servings.

Pumpkin Mac and Cheese

Yield: about 6 cups
Prep 30 mins
Bake 30 mins
Stand 10 mins

Ingredients:

2 cups dried elbow macaroni
2 tablespoons butter
2 tablespoons all-purpose flour
1/2 teaspoon salt
1/2 teaspoon ground black pepper
1 cup whipping cream
1 cup whole milk
1 15 - ounce can pumpkin
1 cup shredded Fontina cheese (4 ounces)
1 tablespoon snipped fresh sage or 1/2 teaspoon dried sage, crushed
1/2 cup soft bread crumbs
1/2 cup grated Parmesan cheese
1/3 cup chopped walnuts
1 tablespoon olive oil
Fresh sage leaves (optional)

Directions:

1. Preheat oven to 350 degrees F. In a large saucepan cook macaroni according to package directions; drain. Return cooked macaroni to hot saucepan; cover and keep warm.

2. Meanwhile, for cheese sauce, in a medium saucepan heat butter over medium heat until melted. Stir in flour, salt, and pepper. Gradually stir in whipping cream and milk. Cook and stir until slightly thickened and bubbly. Stir in pumpkin, fontina cheese, and the snipped fresh or dried sage until cheese is melted. Pour cheese sauce over cooked macaroni; stir gently to coat. Transfer mixture to a 2-quart rectangular baking dish.

3. For crumb topping, in a small bowl combine bread crumbs, Parmesan cheese, walnuts, and oil; sprinkle over macaroni mixture. Bake about 30 minutes or until macaroni mixture is bubbly and crumb topping is golden. Let stand for 10 minutes before serving. If desired, garnish with sage leaves.

Lobster Macaroni and Cheese

Prep 35 mins
Bake 30 mins
Stand 10 mins

Ingredients:

12 ounces dried mini bow tie pasta or mini penne pasta
6 slices apple wood-smoked bacon
3 cups sliced fresh cremini mushrooms (8 ounces)
2 medium leeks, sliced (2/3 cup)
8 ounces cooked lobster meat,* chopped
8 ounces process Gruyere cheese, cut up
1 1/2 cups half-and-half or light cream
1 cup crumbled blue cheese (4 ounces)
1 tablespoon truffle-flavor oil
1/8 teaspoon cayenne pepper
1 1/2 cups coarse soft bread crumbs (2 slices)
1 tablespoon butter or margarine, melted

Directions:

1. Preheat oven to 350 degrees F. Grease a 3-quart rectangular baking dish; set aside. Cook pasta according to package directions; drain. Return to pan.

2. Meanwhile, in a large skillet cook bacon over medium heat until crisp. Drain bacon on paper towels, reserving 2 tablespoons drippings in skillet. Crumble bacon; set aside. Add mushrooms and leeks to the reserved drippings; cook about 5 minutes or until tender.

3. Stir crumbled bacon, mushroom mixture, lobster meat, Gruyere cheese, half-and-half, blue cheese, truffle oil, and cayenne pepper into cooked pasta. Transfer mixture to the prepared baking dish.

4. Bake, covered, for 20 minutes. Stir gently. In a small bowl combine bread crumbs and melted butter; sprinkle over pasta mixture. Bake, uncovered, for 10 to 15 minutes more or until mixture is heated through and crumbs are lightly browned. Let stand for 10 minutes before serving.

Lobster Macaroni and Cheese

www.ingramcontent.com/pod-product-compliance
Lightning Source LLC
Chambersburg PA
CBHW041232040426
42444CB00002B/134